our lady of perpetual degeneracy

by robin gow

tolsun books
flagstaff, arizona & las vegas, nevada

Our Lady of Perpetual Degeneracy

Copyright © 2020 by Robin Gow. All rights reserved. Printed in the United States of America. First Edition. For more information, contact Tolsun Books at info@tolsunbooks.com.

Edited by Heather Lang-Cassera.

Cover art and design by David Pischke.

No part of this book may be used or reproduced in any manner whatsoever without the prior written permission of the copyright holder except for brief quotations in critical articles or reviews.

Set in Garamond 12 pt font.
Design by David Pischke.

ISBN 978-1-948800-34-1

Published by Tolsun Books, LLC
Flagstaff, Arizona & Las Vegas, Nevada
www.tolsunbooks.com

I began to feel the pleasure of the weightless state between here and there.

                                        Leslie Feinberg, *Stone Butch Blues*

contents

invocation	iii
escape	iv
blue	vi
vows of virginity	viii
two glasses of water	x
sacrament	xii
bride of christ	xiii
on eating	xvi
creed	xix
chrism & stir fry & grill	xxii
churches of geel	xxv
the will of god	xxvi
temples of venus	xxviii
cock	xxv
choke me	xxxii
some stations of the cross	xxxv
sacrament	xxxvii
hair	xxxviii
the birds	xli
sacrament	xliii
weeping statues	xliv
on sleep	xlvi
all saints day	xlix
god heals	li

sacrament	liv
"the great"	lv
some stations of the cross	lvii
the our father	lix
sacrament	lxii
our heads	lxiii
our lady of perpetual degeneracy	lxvi
some stations of the cross	lxx
stoning	lxxiii
the sensuous mysteries	lxxiv
sacrament	lxxxvi
the holy spirit	lxxxvii
sacrament	lxxx
40 days	lxxxi
300 christians eaten by lions	lxxxiv
send me some fruits from your bridegroom's garden	lxxxvii
st. nicholas	xc
magic tricks	xcii
swim lessons	xciv
some stations of the cross	xcviii
i played elijah in my church's vacation bible school theater	ci

our lady of perpetual degeneracy

invocation
glory be to the farther, the spun, & the holy women
as it wasn't in the beginning & now shall be
world with innumerable ends

escape

heaven: house at
the end of the street,
bigger on the inside than out.
a front door. a lock.
st. peter born again & again
into the body of a jack russell terrier.
jesus feeds him bones beneath
the kitchen table. he barks
angrily when people arrive too
early. purgatory, the freshly
mowed front lawn. everything
is domestic, but especially violence.
oh god of love
oh god of mercy &
the broom handle & heavy
granite fingers.
oh god of love
oh god of mercy &
blue the color of bruises.
what is to be assumed of
a powerful man who demands
worship is just about always true.
call him lord or yahweh or father,
he will find a way to hurt you.
halos hung on the coat rack,
all the lay people in the attic,
mary, again, tucking jesus
into the cabinet below the sink,

putting her finger to her lips.
hold your breath
while he passes.
his steel-toe boots by the door.
his hunger & the kitchen table.
his flickering love in the form
of newly created flowers
in a mason jar on the table.
fear is the color white.
what no one suspected
was her to leave that sunday night.
the table all set.
holy mary mother of god
having laid down each place for each
person & angel, the innumerable all.
our mother ran with only a backpack
full of roses. her halo
still on the towel rack. she wouldn't
need it anymore.
earth, strangely warm & grey.
ambling through the bethesda terrace
in central park she laughed
at how much she had missed
having a ground-touching body. on the lip
of the foundation, standing a step taller,
pressing her hands together & praying.

blue

this morning i ran my body
78 sidewalk squares wide,
around & around passing
a plastic front lawn statue
of st. mary. (our mother).
on each pass the house's
automatic lights would
blink on & she would be
posed different.
there she is kneeling
on the stoop, cigar in between
fingers. i stopped &
asked her what she was
doing here on long island.
she stood up, slithering
over to me, something
uncanny about the motions
of her body. we went behind
the laundromat where
all the pigeons trade gossip.
i told her i was worried
that my only
faith occurs when i run,
my sweat wet hair chilly
in the grey air. she tells
me she gave it up,
everything to be here.
she gestures down at

her feet & the snake
that she's usually stepping on
now coiled as an anklet.
staring up at me, he winked.
we sat closer together
on the back stoop
& she held out her arm
to me, tracing her veins
with one finger & prompting
me to touch. her skin,
winter metal.
blue blood to match.
i mapped my own pulse,
warm & rushing.
what a human, what i wouldn't
give to be only flesh again.
the snake, kissing my neck.
the punishment for turning
away from a strong man
is always reptilian
even if he is your son.

vows of virginity

last night st. lucy came
to my door & knocked three times.
the mother the daughter
& the holy bedpost that i use
as a rosary.

running out of veneration,
she sat at my desk chair,
placing each scented-candle of
her crown on the end table.
rose & cream & patchouli & lavender.

i asked her what she was
doing here so far from december
& she put a finger to my mouth.
her eyes looking up from the golden
plate, unblinking. white grape.
for broken vows
& pagan boys we never loved.
for the stained glass
on the brothel walls
we made a curtain. she told
me of bundles of wood
& fire that only women know.
she danced her fingers
over flame to demonstrate.

i stuck out my tongue,
the taste her ember as
sweet wine. eyeball in her
palm she fed me,
yes both eyes, off the plate.
juice down my neck,
across my collar bones.

she asked for my confessions,
turning them into pastries
on her plate. tea cakes
& macaroons. the powdered
sugar on our lips.

we will take this all
to the catacombs.
diocletian, a statue outside
the window. he's dead now,
we know. but a man is
always a statue left somewhere.
i asked her if her
eyes would grow back
& already there
was another pair.
blue & lucid.

two glasses of water

i mistook a thump in the basement
for the washing machine on its
last spin cycle. iphone flashlight out,
i crept down the wooden stairs
to find st. gabriel & st. michael
sitting on the cool cement floor.
they were so bright, all over,
skin made of neon, only,
less harsh & more like honey.
their hands were full of feathers,
dropping from their wings.
michael, with their arms cradling
feathers, a dying child,
i brought them trash bags to
clean the plumage up &
glasses of water because i did not
know what angels drink.
they poured the water on each
other, kissed necks,
caressed faces. came around me,
pressed lips to my forehead.
bodies the texture of soft stone.
i invited them upstairs but they
declined, scared of walking earth
where god could see them
full of glimmering lust.
now each day when i wake up
& when i go to bed

i bring them two glasses
of water. they crawl into
the washing machine
& thump
& pray.

sacrament

& all the faucets pour oil or milk.
we fill father's bottles, the brown & green;
thick glass blood-cells, a throat-slit pouring silk.
when will the baptisms make me feel clean?

we dig holes in the yard. they fill with mud.
i go, i drop in all the shiny things,
the necklaces clit-plucked, pink flower bud,
my hole amuck mess: gargling glint rings.

our dish soap is blue & so is mary.
she's plastic bottle, she's soil bubble.
it's baby bath, she rubs me black cherry.
we go digging for the pit, pair knuckle.

& so, i repeat, each morning again.
stain skin, sugary with original sin.

bride of christ

people with the same name
easily fall in love with each other.

catherines; of siena & alexandria
wearing white cowls & wedding dresses,
one rising, one drying the plates
i'd left over in the sink.

the purple sponge. siena,
turning her hands over in the hot
water till they were red,
the stigmata coming off like
ink marker, down the drain,
all the years of bleeding.
alexandria kissing them,
telling her she was
a good wife,
she was *the best wife*.

the wedding bands,
simple gold,
i ask to hold them.

in high school when i loved
a boy & thought i was a girl
i would sometimes look
at bridal magazines,
mythologizing a wedding.

it wasn't that i wanted
to marry him but that
i wanted a photograph-able
future, the shapes of dresses:
the mermaid, the ball gown—
pearls & lace

i do,
i tell the catherines
*i do love you
in a way a god couldn't*

& they start to weep,
only instead of milk or tears
purple streaks down their faces

we laugh & the colors
change, from purple to blue
to red, not a blood red
but a scarlet garnet—
the kind of blood girls
without gods get to have,

divorced women,
the wedding bands down
the sink's throat.

the kitchen floor
dripping with color
like oil spill rain

we finger paint
their dresses, they kiss
me, leaving purple
& gold lip prints
on my face & my shoulders

i leave them, holding
each other on the counter

i do i do i do i do

i don't wash the
marks off before bed—

what a mess what a mess

on eating

the doctor's hands were cold
on my breasts. in a tall mirror
at the corner of the examining
room i glanced & saw another
angle of us. i thought
this is another person,
not me.
strange figure ghost.

in the mirror i also saw
st. agatha sitting in
a folding chair by the bed

& when the doctor exited
she came over to also
feel my chest.

her own breasts torn off
with hot pincers by
a flock of unknowably
angry men

she carried them,
her breasts, with
her on a golden plate:
two chiffon cakes;
beautiful, almost porcelain,
& unmaimed.

as she touched me she told
me that she understands,
that making a body feel alive
is a process

we ate each one of her
breasts from the plate,

she brought plastic forks.

mine tasted like
strawberry angel food &
she said that hers tasted
like peach nectar,
but also that they're
always different,
each day another confection.

wiping crumbs off of our
thighs we traded stories
about our chests & about
men taking handfuls of them—

she asked if we could lay down
together on the examining table
& presses me into it.

the crinkle of wax paper
made me feel like an orb

of hard candy; butterscotch maybe.
her tongue dripping across my neck,
taking handfuls of me like cake.

i whisper to her about
how sorry i am that i want
to cut off my breasts & that
she had no say about how they
ripped off hers.

she kisses the apology out of me
& leaves before the surgeon comes back.

tell me,
do we share the same body?

creed

the church assembly stands, mouths open like
syrup cruets, ladle lip & spoon.

i believe in god,
the father almighty,
creator of heaven and earth,

the video of this plays,
projected on the far wall of my bedroom,
i stand again & again,
mouth opening & words coming out,
whose words?

i carve in my thigh with a letter-opener
to rebuke them,

i believe in Her
i believe Her
the trauma, un-bind me
we shutter heaven & earth

this, the night after
brett kavanaugh was confirmed
to the supreme court.

and in jesus christ, his only son, our lord,
who was conceived by the holy spirit,
born of the virgin mary,

*suffered under pontius pilate,
was crucified, died and was buried;*

& it makes sense to me why god
had to kill his son, the boy hiding now
beneath the sink, we call him jesus

a world has to be founded on
the pain of a man because pain
of a woman or a queer is never believed

an uncrucified body isn't suffering.

*he descended into hell;
on the third day he rose again from the dead;
he ascended into heaven,*
i kneel down & bring the boy
oreos, the golden kind. he blesses
them, he says *this is our body*
& feeds me

*and is seated at the right hand of god the father almighty;
from there he will come to judge the living and the dead.*

we come to sit on my bed,
make shadow puppets of the projection
as the voices keep speaking,

i kiss his forehead & tell him
i believe in us

i believe in the holy spirit,

the holy catholic church,
the communion of saints,
the forgiveness of sins,

making a shadow of a hawk,
i land on his shoulder, i tell
him that we're not safe & that
the saints can't be prayed to anymore,

he makes his hand talk,
mouthing along to the creed, puppet finger

the resurrection of the body,
and life everlasting.

chrism & stir fry & grill

breakfast-smell has a body:
st. lawrence. pacing the house
& slapping a spatula
against the walls.

his entrance makes everyone
hungry, it's one of his miracles.

he asks why i'm not eating
& i tell him it's because
i don't know what to make.

he says it's time for stir fry,
assembling the ingredients
by the stovetop, i help him,
water chestnuts & leeks &
bok choy & sugar snap peas.

it's late, past midnight
& he insists that no one
in the world can go to sleep
less than full.

i don't keep oil in the kitchen
so we leave to get the chrism
from the glass case at
the back of the church.

i tell him about the bishop
dipping his thumb in oil
to make a cross on my head
to confirm me.

promises to god often
taste like spitting oil
& garlic.

we cry because we're hungry
& because we're blasphemous now.

i touch his scars: great big grill
marks, like a panini press
bit his torso—charred cheeks.

he asks if i know what skin
tastes like & i tell him
that i can make some assumptions.

the patron of grilling
on account of his own body
over the hot coals—
a martyr a martyr

we escape with the chrisms,
the amber tint to the oil &
measure tablespoons into the wok

placing his open palm in the pan
to prove it doesn't hurt,
he invites me to join him
so i do & the churning feels
cathartic. he bites his thumb
but i don't eat my hands
because i'm still vegetarian.

hush & hiss as he stirs,
the rice on the stove.

eating at the breakfast table
late into the night

fork scrape & the big spoon.
st. lawrence says
we still have mouths
we still have mouths

churches of geel

dymphna oh duchess oh diaphragm,
her severed head clutched in her hand.

this is for girls who father each other, one to another,
a hallway, sinew smothered in *sorry*.

pacing the street, blue called her feet.
i comb her to couch & she carries me.

doll limp & licorice, we share siloes of
men's lips, wedding fathers, blood slips

down legs. i ask her what churches she
keeps now the geel is gone & grieve-able

& mad people suck the steeples for air.
where heal the girls when god is done?

what churches, what churches &
lurch the ledge that un-birthed me.

when i want to kill myself i say
st. dymphna oh darling of depress

& derange—we're chewed up & strange,
a church, a church, a pew, a name.

the will of god

i find st. mejella on the back-gravel road
where the neighbors leave

out cantaloupe rinds for the foxes
& where the black beetles leak from soil.

he prays into the corn, shucking
ears & hoping to come upon an infant

inside one. patron to the unborn, i wanted
to ask him if he guards my body

each time i buy pregnancy tests
& wait for the single line telling me

that i'm empty. i draw single lines in
the dirt. i ask him if i swallow

the peach pits & strawberry freckles
& apple seeds if any one of them will curl

up inside me & become human. sinews
& stems. i used to be so scared of it,

swallowing cum & feeling it thrash like
minnows in my throat, the fish assembling

into a body. i spit children into napkins.
st. majella, finding the raw corn,

touching the kernels till they become
fingers. i ask what he does now that

he's left heaven & he says he's been
planting seeds. he remembers my mother,

her blood clotting like bubblegum
when she was pregnant with my brother,

the syringes that huddled in her
closet like a choir; a medical song.

he once revived a boy who fell
from the side of a cliff, yes

miracle that was me, the stone inside
without a heartbeat. a boy in me with a

womb around him, a husk. boil us
tonight in the heat of the moon.

he says that this is all the will of god.
my brother & my mother & the organs that

grew in me like melon. i slice my stomach
i feed the foxes, he sings.

temples of venus

st. afra smacked, pounding nails into wood
& i sleepwalked to where she stood in the yard;
her fishnet stockings, halo snapped into headband.

about a year ago i started touching myself again,
first just a fist over top underwear,
mortar pestle me, i ground into sand, spilled

out my window. she's rebuilding the temples of venus
like the one where she used to be a hierodule.
a sacred sex slicer, a shrine shaking

slut like me. she says she can't believe
she ever sealed off her clit for god, for christ.
laughing we make sacrifices to her,

the love goddess, chopping my dildos
sideways & pouring lubes into basins,
oh holy mother water. no ivory columns here,

just a tree house. a ladder dangling
that i climb with my lover. we make sacred
our queer bodies. i show her how

i touch myself & st. afra dresses
us in fishnets, roses blooming where
we once had genitals, the scent of evergreen,

the altar where our blood comes out white.
myrtles pollen pucker our throats, she prays
for us, that we find pleasure there.

cock

hurling rocks at the front door,
st. peter stood at the end of driveway in his slippers,
the last to leave, fury-weeping & red-faced.

he remembers the cocks, screeching
two times & himself denying god out of fear,
hoping his life would burn up in that sun.

the roosters lay eggs this time,
i fill my pockets with them, they're
heavy with all of st. peter's guilt,

the rocks
on which he builds churches
on which he built a fist-made god
on which he clenched body so
tight that the fish around his boat
turned granite & sank.

on which he prayed to wrath
until it festered into a body,
a throne-man like we all have known,

his chicken bones on the dining room floor
without the saint women to wash & clean.

we throw the eggs, shells smashing
on the windows, one shattering glass.
the glass becoming egg shell, the egg shell

becoming *stained* glass, red & blue & green
& autumn yellow——the cocks laying oranges
made of glass——shards or feathers?

our cocks crow, loud & confused.
what is a man then if he renounces everything?
if his god has been a god of hurt.

if brotherhood is gravel & always leaves
the mouth dry & bleeding.

what is to be salvaged in a screaming cock?

i take mine off & put it in the drawer
with the rest of the rubber dildos

st. peter's gets louder & louder
& louder——an alarm clock——a red-flicker siren,
a plague.

the rooster's eggs are all yolk,
no whites at all. i crack one over
my head & it runs down my back,
griddle sizzling on down spine——

the roosters give me green shiny feathers.
i tell them i'm some kind of man,
though i'm not sure what kind yet.

choke me

dragon's tail & flog,
he tests them first on his
own forearm, a careful dom

the ceiling fixture becoming
wick to drip hot wax down our backs.

i tell st. blaise about how monsignor
crossed the candles at our throats.

may almighty god at the intercession
of st. blaise, bishop & martyr,
preserve you from infections of the throat
& from all other afflictions

a yawn becoming a rash,
swallowing glass,

the words that have stood
on my teeth like bridge jumpers.

i tell him i want him to choke me.

our safe word is *water.*

his coarse fingers, sturdy as
my father's.

liberation is to be in control for once.

be the master of
how & where you're
deprived of air,

alone on the floor with
a floral neck tie i never wear,

temporary asphyxiation, a scarf

the sick animals find us,
smack against the window,

the pigeons & palm-size sidewalk birds,
grey rabbits & splotchy tabby cats

circling the bed, they claw us
& we love it, the teeth of it all.

i can't heal you anymore
he pleas.

i have no more miracles.

i wipe his tears
with the sheet, they're hot &
dry like wax.

i dig my nails in his back,

a climax of leather,
cuffed to the bed post,
red-wrist me lover,

here & now is
where i want to be bound.

what is pain when prayed for?

some stations of the cross

1.
leaving
wash your hands before
leaving this room. the pipes have
no water for you. wash your hands before
leaving. the pipes want you.
stick your toe in first, the entry point.
you will fit.

2.
ellipsis
the skipped stone keeps going, out
the front door & out your mouth,
i follow it, i follow it like a rainbow or
the phone line silence where my father
forgets what fathers are supposed to say.
eating them like breadcrumbs, there is
no way back, just the stone getting somewhere
un-arrive-able.

3.
orgy
the basket of hot peaches we picked
& ate too quickly. bruised & soft, it had to be done.
so many of them. the room is crowded & i keep
repeating everyone's names to keep track.
i me you she he they
i he she you
whose hand is turning my stem?
whose nectar?

4.
worship
the dick almighty. the surgeon almighty with
his catherine-wheel of dicks. they grow out of
the ceiling like chandeliers. beautiful dicks.
blooming dicks. the dick in the tabernacle.
eucharistic-dick, melting beneath my tongue.

am i a boy now?

sacrament

we open cabinets; walk fridge-white walls.
licking the floor for salt; jesus, crawls in
the mixing bowl, spoon in his mouth, he calls
for his father to feed him. he has been

the good stove-top son; pressing his hand flat
down on the cutting board, paring fingers
& making wafers. this time, slice my fat,
call me bacon strip & bone broth bringer.

as i cook i apologize that i
once dropped eucharist on the church floor.
the boy giggles, shows the bruise on his thigh
from the fall. plate body; give back the gore.

his fork planting ellipsis in my arm;
stigmata fry me till my meat is firm.

hair

barefoot on the porch
i find her,
hair following her like a wedding train.

st. clair tells me she can see the ghosts
of people's hair & that mine is so long
that it goes down the basement steps.

i rub her feet till she can feel them again.
she also doesn't eat meat & so
we have microwave veggie burgers;
chickpea & pesto.

her hair keeps growing & she tells
me that she hates it, that she hates
how long she's let it grow.

the more upset, the more it swells—
great curls & loops & knots.

i tell her that i want to help her
cut it off & she says that she cut it
first for god

after she left she wanted it to grow
so that someone new might want to
love her.

no one new came,

hair monstrous & un-tamable.

she kneels over the waste basket
& i get out the hair clippers,
the gentle buzzing across scalp.
as i shave her hair it turns into milk,

droplets in the sink
just like mine on the floor
of the salon.

the first time i shaved my hair short
it felt like peeling all the boys' fingers
off of my skull, all the times
men had yanked,
made leashes of me,
turned fatty & liquid.

we finish &
her head is bristly,
an early june peach.

i tell her she needs to shave
mine too, closer this time.

i tell her to take off the top
layer of skin,

plum red & vein.

she digs pits from my skull,

so many for one fruit,
her fingers stained & bloody.

she keeps apologizing as she

drops them in the trash.

i ask about my ghost hair
& she says not to worry about it
so i ask again & she admits
that it's so long that it
dips in the ocean, fondles
the seaweed on the north shore.

closing my eyes
i feel the light pull.

she holds me.

i say
i want it off—
i want it off

the birds

day & night st. francis preaches to the birds in my yard. they tilt their heads & blink dead-eyed & blank. he opens the book of psalms, singing for the birds. st. francis has the voice of a songbird, he trades throats with robins & nuthatches. it doesn't work like it used to. the birds don't listen. they go about their business. the birds buy stocks. the birds eat from twinkie wrappers. the birds push their children out of the nests too early.

when billy & i would play in the park he was convinced that if he tried hard enough he could catch a bird. dad said if he succeeded we could keep it. he would dart back & forth, arms extended. the birds always just out of reach.

st. francis takes the stale ends of bread, rubs them in his hands till they crumble. the walls of a cathedral. he feeds the birds from his hands. they don't talk to him. they avert their stares.

in my dreams we catch a bird finally. it is an unruly bird with blueberries for eyes—its eyes keep falling out so we wash them in the sink & eat them. the bird, angry with my brother & i, chases us to the far end of the park where all the benches are broken & the trees are too old to remember each other's names.

st. francis crawls into dad's workshop in the basement. his bare feet are cold on the hard cement floor. the pipes crack & startle him. i sit & watch him working from the stairs. i am eight. i am aware that one shouldn't try to catch birds. he's building houses for them, hundreds of bird houses, all lined in rows.

billy & i liked to paint bird houses, we'd get them premade from acemore or michael's craft store. we'd get a set of primary colors, lay the newspaper out on the kitchen table & paint. we'd dip our hands in paint, stamping them on each other too.

he hangs all the birdhouses from my porch & i tell him
that's too many birdhouses
but he just pretends not to hear me.

he sits, watching out the window from the couch. he drinks peppermint tea. he eats a bagel with jelly on it. i ask him if he needs anything else & he shakes his head. *just the birds.*

of all the birdhouses we made we never actually put any outside. they just sit in the attic or on our bookshelves. ghost birds crawl inside. they open their mouths & no song comes out because st. francis took their voices. i tell him that he should give them back.

the birds all come. all of the birds. every single bird there ever has been. they come. this time they want to preach to him. they ordain each other, the blue jays blessing the catbirds blessing the finches. they put on bishop hats. they don cassocks. they eat bread crumbs & whisper

& this is my body, do this in memory of me.

sacrament

oh, forgive me father for i have sinned
against my gender. call me *traitor, traitor.*
pronoun evader—i'm mâché skinned
& making penance, cut my equator.

so, who do you apologize to now?
god in my jars of white glue & glitter.
i press popsicles to tongues; a pink vow
to always praise-worship my clitoris.

we do macaroni art on plates,
the gold plates where he cuts baby carrots.
hummus hallelujah me! holy waits
for no man, but i'm a green soap spirit!

in confession monsignor paints my nails,
this color suits you, typical for females.

weeping statues

in 2008, church custodian, vincenzo di costanzo, went on trial in northern italy for faking blood on a statue of the virgin mary when his own dna was matched to the blood.

someone has to keep the statues crying;
blood, oil, & water.

mary wakes me up early,
blue cloak over her head,
hands me a ceramic bowl
& tells me to collect my tears
to feed the statues.

all over the world statues
of mary are reported weeping

but almost always proven
hoaxes by church officials.

what they don't know is
st. mary enlists humans,
like me, to tend the statues.

i try different methods
to make myself cry,
imagining my dog dying,
the old playground bulldozed over,
my brother calling me his

sister again out of shame,

the thought maybe all of
this religion was made up to
make us feel better about
the fact that no one knows
what happens after you die.

st. mary shakes her head
& tells me that no one is
allowed to think about that, no one,
not because it's sacrilegious
but because questions
with impending answers
are not worth asking.

i trickle a meager bowl
of tears down the statue
outside my childhood church.
the tears freeze on her face
(a miracle).

afterall, if there was
no afterlife then why
would the statues be weeping?

on sleep

> *I have great love for Saint Joseph, because he is a man of silence and strength. On my table I have an image of Saint Joseph sleeping. Even when he is asleep, he is taking care of the Church!*   pope francis

wake up st. joseph!
i say

he sleeps on the couch all day,

eating all the potato chips
from the cupboard when i'm
away,

        he locks me out,

dips the key in salsa & swallows it

st. joseph, we need you

           wake up!

my father takes a nap after work

      we have a lot of foster fathers
        a whole lot

he drives a blue jeep across the desert

to make batteries in a factory

       at 3am

all fathers are machines of
some sort

    so how come you

can sleep st. joseph?

  all all day

i said *please, please,*
    please

wake up

  i'll do whatever you say.

i'll wear blue for you
    or white

i'll massage your back

  the alarm clock has eight legs

& dangles from the ceiling,
red-eyed & hungry

> go back to sleep, dad
> please, will you sleep in?

& he gets up again,
he keeps getting up

> we should have talked more quietly

i'm hundreds of miles away
& here i am still waking him up

st. joseph, what are you going to do?

the church is a doll house

a plastic stove
a front door
a tiny bell the guests
ring when they arrive

> i'm a plastic doll house joseph

take care of me
i want a father

he just keeps sleeping
he's pretending though, i see him peer at
> me with one sneaky eye

fine, I'll be my father I say

> & i tuck him in

all saints day

all of them,
all the saints,

they can all come out
on the 1st of november

they come dressed up as each other

st. joseph as st. lucy laughing with
two grapes on a plate as eyes,

st. clare as st. francis,
with a fake parrot glued
to her shoulder

st. francis as st. denis,
holding a papier-mâché severed head
full of cherry throat lozenges

st. catherine as the other
st. catherine, everyone pretends that they
can tell them apart but they're so similar
that their costumes don't make
much of a difference

the end of the day
is the best part

all the saints go
house-to-house martyring themselves,
even the ones that didn't have
a chance to be martyred in their
real lives

don't worry,
it's not morbid,

they go up in a poof
of smoke as they do,

the smoke smells like
cotton candy & comes in
all sorts of colors

i was excited when the doorbell rang,
outside, standing st. leo,
my brother's favorite saint

i wanted to invite him in,
but i knew what he was here for

he put a water gun to his
forehead & pulled the trigger

& BAM!

god heals

before there was an earth to look down on
god pulled a fully cooked bird
out of his mouth
tore it into seven pieces

one of those pieces
named himself raphael.

the birth of angels is awkward.

i found him yesterday face up in
the bird bath at the park in fleetwood,
he said to me

> *i want to be a feather*

& i said
    me too

so we splayed ourselves thin.

    we ate air with plastic forks
off of paper plates

    he touched my back
where the wings would go & said

*you would have made a great angel
before all of this.*

i showed him the backstroke in the pool &
he said he can't heal anyone anymore

    his name means
"god heals"

    & heals & heals & heals

we dig in the dirt at the park
until we find my last pair of heels,
    black & sharp

he puts them on & walks
on the rim of the bird bath,

    i say *be careful!*

i tell him that i had a dream where
all the clothing in my closet
was pink. wherever i went

    there were men in pickup trucks
    slowing down to shout at me.

i would run but the sidewalk
would turn into water & gulp me

in headlight.

    we buy a rotisserie chicken
    & float its body in the fountain of
    bethesda

he says
when i used to do this
the bird would come alive again.

it floats, glistening & golden brown
    in its foil boat.

sacrament

how old do you have to be to promise?
"eleven" the bishop says, dressing our
pink puberty bodies. oh, st. thomas
with his doubts. oh, divine come deflower.

if god wants me so bad he can come get
me. "my lord and my god." the chrism kiss
planted acne in my brain, i fishnet
& fuck. this catechism cuck-ing 'miss.'

yes, i once rejected satan. a girl,
yes, but only approximately. white
robe robbing & spilling the yellow oil.
a contract is with nothing without bite.

i write a letter of resignation;
oh lord, this is my confirmation.

"the great"

a body as an entrance & an archway;
st. leo nails his bones to the door frame of my house.
his remains were once curled up like a dog on the front step
    of st peter's basilica.
now he wants to know how great men should be buried,
always moving, digging, hiding the carcass.
he's ashamed of it, with its rotting & cobwebs.

i ask st. leo the great if he feels great in the afterlife
& he says that he sometimes feels like his
lungs are made of gold & that there is no
amount of air that could make him feel less metallic.

he says he wants be called "st. leo the average" now
& i laugh because that's no name for an ex-pope.
he says he dreams of an office job & a stapler &
a red stress-ball to squeeze when he's feeling upset.

leo regrets never kissing a man (or a woman for that matter).
he kisses his hands like we used to at middle school sleepovers;
he uses tongue.

i tell him that he's my brother's confirmation saint
& that everyone had wanted billy to pick st. michael instead.
(leo agrees that st. michael is more heroic).

in my backpack i find him a page of blank white
printer paper & i tell him to lay down on it as i
dump his bones in one by one.

driving three hours i arrive back at my parent's house
where my brother
has a filing cabinet in his old bedroom.

before putting him in between two manila dividers
i ask leo if he would want to kiss me, just to try it once.

he agrees & i climb in.

the inside of a page of printer paper
is similar to the inside of a chalice, all silver
& ankle deep in wine.

he's not good at kissing but i pretend
like he is. he tells me that i'm a great man,
that there's so many greater men than him.

holding him, i tell him that
we can trade every other day. one day he
can be the great & the next i can be.
he thanks me & puts the greatness
over my shoulders like a cape.

i pose in the downstairs bathroom
with all the mirrors. i don't like
the way it looks but it's only for a day.

some stations of the cross

5.
weight
a hallway in the shape of a _____.
my father reaches down & i grab
hold of his hands; he lets me walk
up his legs—a window cleaner,
i clean my father's windows,
rub the rag in circles till everyone
can see our insides. we name the
air between us "simon."

6.
baby wipes
my brother's face covered in chocolate ice cream.
is he your son?
my brother. *quite an age gap.*

he wipes my face with his frog hands, jesus
the little boy with fingers full of spaghetti,
a brother, another brother. i have so many brothers
but i don't get to be one.

i wipe the girl off my face, her skin
a crater-lake of foundation. war paint pigment.

7.
crush
an m&m candy under thumb,
& the ants all die like push pins,

apply pressure. he's bleeding.
a bookcase can be a thumb,
crashing down, spilling all
the never-been-used weight watchers
magazines, trapping my mother beneath
& jesus too. he lays on his
back. he is milk chocolate,
don't hold him too long or too close,
he'll melt.
eat,
you're a good boy.

8.
women
with tears turning into little bouncy balls.
there's a gumball machine where
your heart should be but that's okay
because i have a lot of quarters.
jesus opens his mouth & i put
in the quarters so he'll work a little longer,
like one of those rides at the mall:
an airplane, a school bus, an ice cream truck.
it's harder to cry now—it's the testosterone.
now when i want to cry for jesus i have
to find a paring knife, sacrifice fruit
to the microwave & eat the hot flesh,
burning my tongue i tear up.

the our father

the first boys i had crushes on were all
altar servers too. unsexed in our robes
we doled out the stations:

the bell
the book
the cross

i always wanted to be
the bell; my tongue
a silver clapper,

lend me your mouth.

i got to mass early so that i
could play with matches, light
the candles around the altar.

i asked him if he wanted
to light one too & he said no.

i struck the match across his chest.

he looked at himself
in the tall mirror at
the other end of the sacristy.

we tied our brown cords
around our waists

& when the our father
came all the servers held hands
as we chanted

who art in heaven

wording murky in the air,
acutely aware of the heat
of my palms—made of
sweating matches.

i would worry that they
knew i liked them because
of that heat.
now on some sunday mornings
i open my closet & only find
the white robes,
i remember my size:13

you're still asleep so
i put the robe on & skirt
around the apartment,

ringing myself.

does this count as mass?

my gender somewhere
beneath the garment.

the connotation of altar boys.

the priest holding out his
hands over the bread, the cue
to ring.

sacrament

oh, i want you to vow me wide open.
i, _____, take you, _____, to be my wife/
husband. i crack in half with devotion
& sew gold-motion. kiss my butter knife.

is the sex procreative? do you know
where babies come from? all of them come out
gold rings. a glinting cervix now aglow
with tulle & mitosis. there is no doubt

i am lawfully & awfully bound
to the wife-husband organs that i have.
i take them out; fill fruit baskets around
the house. a reception for many halves.

i write my own promises all wedding night
to try & make my suture-body right.

our heads

all these centuries,
st. dymphna has traveled,
cradling her severed head
like the child she never got to be,
just to end up on my doorstep,
not knowing what to do with it.

she presents the thing to me,
her head, like a fruit basket
or a soccer ball.

i turn it over & marvel
at how unchanged
her features are—no rot just
some dirt smudges
from sitting beside her
on the railroad.

first, we toss her head back &
forth in my tiny backyard
while she tells me about
her father & how he tried
to marry her himself.
his fat gold-rimmed fingers.

she had looked like
her mother

as we all do.

she ran away only
to be caught & beheaded.

second, we try
to use it to plant tomatoes,
sprinkle seed on the tongue
& shut the mouth,
watching in hopes
that the stalk would
burst from between
her strands of brown hair.

i tell her that i've read
about her & the church
of geel that bloomed
where she died, the waters there
that used to heal mad people like me
& how they knocked it
down to make room for a city.

i ask her where i should
take my body
once my head is off like hers.

she recalls a prayer i made
to her
two decembers ago

the match sticks
i swallowed like seeds.

the paring knife
making new lips
on my forearms.

third, we take my father's
rusty shovel & bury
her head behind the garage
where all the pets are buried:
the turtle & the chick &
the colony of goldfish.

& from that spot
the churches of geel
start growing
like mushrooms

all over the yard

small & edible.

her body falls &
is engulfed by them.

i kiss each roof & say
thank you

our lady of perpetual degeneracy

i started in the morning
with just my backpack, full of
only apples & two peanut butter
granola bars. i left to find mary,
to coax out her apparition.
i walked ocean & highway,
the earth a rubber ball beneath me.

I.
loudes, france
a half-sized statue in the mouth
of the cave like a tongue ring.
i crouched down, touched her stone face.

bernadette soubirous,
who first saw mary here
& mistook her for a woman,
tells me that there's
nothing anymore, that she
wonders if she had ever seen her here.

we draw mary using chalk,
her outline on the cave walls.

II.
guadalupe, mexico
mother moon goddess, the snake
in between toes, the scent
of roses in her basilica.

i sit in a pew next to juan diego
who mary spoke to on his
way to tepeyac. he shushes me.
he's tearing out the pages of
a hymnal & they're turning
into petals.

III.
fatima, italy
when i arrived all the peasant children
were crawling on each other's shoulders;

the acrobatics of forming the shape of a great
giant mary.

the others build a great big fire
in the street. they praise it as
the sun, they say *milagre do sol*

& i ask where mary is
& they point to the mass of children.

IV.
degeneracy, in my bedroom
i return as the sun is setting
& everything is orange &
everyone is orange

i resist the urge to pray
because i don't know who
i would pray to &

that's when they comes.
the click of tall red heels on
the hardwood floor,
the sick sweet smell of
papaya perfume

she's so much orange
that i can't look at him & i sob
& ask them not to hurt me.

his fishnets glow,
hot copper wires

she's an algorithm
of godless energy

carrying two buckets
of oil that he pours
on the floor, all rainbow
& river

they're everything but
an apparition & touching
them is painful, but i have to
do it. she's wearing

a bright pink strap-on
even though they has a dick
of his own.
she doesn't fuck me though,
they just stare at me & laugh
until i laugh too.

he wraps me in an orange
feather boa that turns into
a real snake & slithers
in the oil.

they tells me to touch myself
& i say that i don't know if i can.

some stations of the cross

9.
three
tadpoles left. the grapes
we put in the fish tank & watched,
hatching into small gods & eating
each other as they grew up. this is
family. the back legs come first—
the gills peeling off as orange slices.
down to two tadpoles & then one.
the big one. greedy & beautiful.
i want to be one of the ones that he ate,
a wriggling hopeful amphibian.

10.
strip-
tease, you don't ask me to take
off my clothing. i tape candy bar
wrappers across my nipples so
this isn't obscene. god goes
through phases with his candy,
snickers & reeses cups & then crunch bars.
his chewing is loud & unreasonable.
the chocolates melt all over my hands.
we stop at a gas station & god lays me
on the counter to be unwrapped.
a soft caramel, maybe. a cherry
throat lozenge.

strip
me. make a thrift store of
everything that's ever touched my body.
call it a chapel. say mass
for the sundresses.

11.
nail
gun at the fridge door. no one
is getting in here. this is where we keep
everything forever. a safe 36 degrees.
are you a fahrenheit girl? i am
i think. call me on your celsius phone,
i won't pick up. i'm too busy keeping
our food safe. strangers could come,
hungry & eating. i put hammers in
the flower vases. they bloom.

12.
dyes;
blue & pink & lavender & purple.
you ask me what color you should
dye your hair & i say "on the cross."
it's a beautiful color, but better suited
for sons. it is all easier when we
assume that fathers make sons
to deliberately not save them. this was
all part of the prophecy. he makes

& makes & makes & we bleach out
our brown hair in the sink in the hopes
we'll come out with no history.
bleach the father away. i will
be no god's sacrifice.

stoning

our church used to have a deacon before the diocese sent
him away to another parish. his voice was wobbly & strange
when he'd sing the closing blessing. my brother & i would laugh
& imitate his voice on the way home from church.
we saw him once at the diner up the street. he sat
on an open bible, cupping a bowl full of pea soup,
the steam fogging his glasses. he fished stones
out of the green broth, gifts from st. stephen.
when i find stones in my own cups of tea & cereal bowls
i throw them away. i tell him that i don't want
to be a deacon. it's his job to recruit deacons
& he does so with stones. it's very persuasive, you see,
because i'm always careful, making sure not to
eating too hurriedly. st. stephen wears the rocks
on his shoulders like parrots, relics from his heroic death
by stoning: the violent tendencies of nature grow round
& angry. i make pea soup & the old deacon arrives
at my breakfast table. he says that he remembered me
& my brother, that he saw us laughing in our mom's
blue station wagon. i tell him i'm sorry for making
fun of his voice all those sundays. he sings
in latin & i laugh & the stones break through
the windows & pile on top of the both of us.

the sensuous mysteries

the last time i prayed the rosary it was for a boy i went on two
    dates with.
his name was joseph, the father, but everyone called him joey.
i told him i loved him because he was a good catholic boy.
    he lived in
a clean house with his twin brother who was also named joseph.

mary gave st. dominic the first rosary all those years ago,
she kissed him hard & pulled the necklace from his throat,
glinting with spit & blood. he washed it off in the river
& put it around his followers' necks,
praying them, making them beads.

joey had begged me to say the rosary for him,
kissed my feet. pleaded.
he believed if a girl like me prayed
he would arrive safe in italy on his family's vacation.

& so, on my bedroom floor, i took each bead
in between my fingers—the words turning potluck
under my tongue—stew & pearled.

i summoned st. dominic by accident,
an odd looking, 11th century man, partially bald.
he had big hands & pale skin. he stared at me blankly
from the bottom of my bunk bed, leaning down
to kiss each bead as he prayed it.

i had wanted to kiss joey, not because i loved him
but because i wanted to make a rosary out of him,
because i wanted to make a body out of him
divide him into five decades:
the joyful mysteries
the sorrowful mysteries
the glorious mysteries
the luminous mysteries

when i finished i looked st. dominic
in the eyes & asked if we could add another decade,
the sensuous mysteries & without hesitation
he took out purple plastic beads from
his robe pockets & started to string them on,

we prayed the decade together till
i came. each hail mary a finger
on my body—close with the our father,
the joseph & his twin joseph,
the plane landing like a great big cross.

sacrament

when i was little, i asked mom how sick
someone had to be to get anointed.
i asked again at fourteen; match-stick-thick-
boned-me, dying & brass doorknob jointed.

go forth, christian soul; gave my own last rites
in the fogged medicine cabinet mirror.
go in peace selfish thing. i flew three kites
for lightning. *this cream makes a face clearer*,

i said, applying the oils to skin;
reflection in the baptismal fountain.
saints! come meet her/him, beautiful/thin.
is death the sacrament then? god pounding

at my double doors. inside there's kitchen
& a fryer to make a good christian.

the holy spirit

i buy a packet of basil seeds from the hardware store
& plant them in an emptied yogurt container full
of soil. i think of the times in the summer
when my mother would try to grow a basil plant,
again, plucking the fresh leaves & burying
her face in them saying *smell them, so fresh*.
i am planting them because i want to find
st. basil to ask him about the holy spirit.

he sprouts quickly & sits in the kitchen sink
with a metal pot full of ingredients.
he appreciates the pun. he picks out a handful
of basil leaves & says *smell them, so fresh*.

i tell him how in sunday school the catechist
brought a bag of feathers, cupped one in her hand
& blew. the feather fell to the floor & she
said that the holy spirit was the air & then
listed on the chalkboard
light, water, fire, dove.
all the ways we find the holy spirit.

st. basil gets up & arranges the kitchen,
he says *we need to eat*. i sit on the counter,
younger than i had expected myself to be.

he spent his whole life in search of the holy ghost
& all he can tell me is that we have to cook,

lights the gas stove & says *fire*
sets a pot to boil & says *water*
pulls a dead bird out & says *dove*

he instructs me to pluck its feathers,
each one turning into a basil leaf as i do.
he collects them. he says *caprese*
& slices the fresh white mozzarella *light*
& slices the thick tomatoes *fire*.

i don't have matching plates in my apartment
so we eat off of paper ones. i admit to him
that i never understood the holy spirit
& what it was supposed to be doing.

he says *you should cook*.
i laugh because i should.
he climbs in between two slices of
the cheese & tomato. i drizzle
extra-virgin olive oil all over his face,
it gets in his beard.

i feed him bites of the dove's tender meat.
i expected it to be like chicken but it's
more like duck. i tell him
that i can't eat it because i'm vegetarian

& he says but you have to
or i can't go in peace.

so i put the flesh in my mouth,
tuck it under my tongue
until he crawls back into
the soil. i spit the dove-meat
out but there's nothing there.

sacrament

sing me into celibacy circus;
i write sermons in purple sidewalk chalk.
holy means *set apart for some purpose*.
i preach naked so i'm easy to *clock*.

the 34 red archbishops travel
to arrest me for mocking the priesthood
but they're scared of this strange-gender mammal.
i eat handfuls of gravel & pew-wood.

i could be a great *trans*itional dia-
conate if they let me. what a body
i'd be, skipped seminary, *ave maria!*
they can't exer these schisms; it's all me.

there were no holy orders for women
or queers, so we made poems, thrived hidden.

40 days

st. medardus laughed all of his teeth out
& they turned into raindrops, pattering on
the hood of my car in the parking lot
outside my dorm building.

i had a strange summer,
living on my college's campus
after i'd graduated.
the world was a fabulous ghost
& i took to worshipping fireflies
like unnamed martyrs.

st. medardus found
my life intriguing
& watching it made him unable
to stick to his convictions.
it was like a reality tv show,
he saw me as a plotless character.
how lovely.

whatever the weather is
like on his feast day, june 8th,
it's supposed to continue for
40 days, but this year was
so abnormal that he found
little reason to keep with traditions.

he sat crossed legged
in the clouds; a man made of weather
& mischief, painting storms
whenever i had a lover
come over.

i'd meet each boy,
across the parking lot
& i want him to love me
forever, but only hypothetically.
we would have grey clouds
as children & move to a small town
in pennsylvania with cul-de-sacs.

one boy painted his finger nails blue & purple
(like all boys should).
i took him up to my bed to test
the size of the room,
the eyelid of
the thin rectangle window
pulled shut & we laid
inside damp & divided pupils.

in the clouds st. medardus
tried the color mauve on
his own nails, no longer
feeling the need to be masculine
with no god looking over his shoulder.

the storm swelled
outside as we laid together
& he told me that he loved thunderstorms
& i said that i did too.

i knew st. medardus watched
us making love,

he did so similar
to how one might look
at a nude renaissance painting,
stroking his beard &
pondering the shape
of bodies.

300 christians eaten by lions

before bed, mom read to us from
the big book of catholic saints
& as she read, she'd summon them,
guests in our room but
always pretend not to see them.

i was the top-bunk sibling
so, they got in bed with billy.

he shared his blankets, always
the more generous sibling.

there was st. ambrose
who leaned his staff against the bedpost
& st. cyricus who was just
a child, younger than us.
he asked for a midnight snack
& we got him milano cookies.

the night that was most memorable
though was the night when we read
about the 300 christians who
were eaten by lions in rome.

is that all someone has to do
to become a saint?
i had asked as the christians
started to file in the door
of our room.

they died for god, they
gave everything up,
she said.

to myself, i thought about
how boring a story that was.

of course, the christians
were quite perturbed that
i didn't find being eaten
an adequate sacrifice,
they showed us their scars &
their maimed flesh, all
packed tightly together
in the small room
as my mother read aloud
their story.

i didn't hear the details
over the commotions
of the christians,
some of who climbed
up to my bunk because
there was so little room.

pulling the blanket
over my head i thought for
a moment
that i should go out & find a place

to be killed for god
so that i could go to heaven.

but i wasn't like the christians.

i knew deep inside that
i would be eaten by many creatures
& none of those would ever
make me a martyr.

send me some fruits from your bridegroom's garden
a pagan lawyer in the trial against st. dorothea of caesarea

when they cut off
st. dorothea's head it fell
off & became a basket of apples,
different types each time:
golden delicious & mcIntosh
& winesap & macoon.

this process repeats itself.
continuously she's filling & refilling
the ceramic bowl
on the kitchen table in
my parents' house.

they don't eat fruit fast
enough.

when i visit some
have always gone rotten.

there wasn't enough
proof that st. dorothea was
a real person so in 1969
they removed her from
the calendar of feasts.

i tell her when i see her
stocking the produce aisle
that i believe in her
more than god.

each year on her old
feast day she brings
buckets of apples,
all of which came from
her head being chopped off,
dumping them at the vatican.

the nuns there use them
for pie, which they
eat in secret at night, not
sharing with the brothers.

my first job was at
an apple orchard & alone
as i picked fruit
i would talk to her

& she'd pinch the branches
to make the apples grow.

i'd eat nothing but
apples all day, right
through the cores,
chewing the stems.

last night, she brought
me my favorite type,
mutzu; green & as big
as baby heads, a whole
basket full.

they were crying so
we cut them up.

she told me this year
she wouldn't be going
to the vatican, that
we would make our own
pies & the holy people
could come to us & beg
her to be a saint again.

st. nicholas

I. coins

i'm not good at budgeting.

i feel like 20-something-year-olds
should have enough money to
buy everyone something fantastic
for christmas.

for dad, i would have
a team of saints go build
him a shed in the backyard,
complete with a wood stove
& a soft yellow lamp.

st. nicholas keeps
dropping bags of gold in through
my window.

i can't take this i say
& pour the coins out on
the porch for the birds to eat.

he's taken a liking to me,
he's always looking for someone
to save. aren't we all?

i appreciate him though
because he tries to save people

without killing his son
(looking at you god).

i don't have a son
or a sack of gold
or even a shed.

in his oldest legend
he dropped bags of gold
in a father's window to
help him pay his
daughter's dowry
"saving them from
prostitution."
when i fucked men
for money i felt like
each time i was finally
saving myself, like
i could pull coins
out of my vagina.
my room had
no windows.

take them, take them
st. nicholas says
from outside the window,
his breath fogging the glass.

II. shoes

each year on st. nicholas day
mom would tell us to put
our shoes out on the porch:
my ratty light-up black & red boy's sneakers.

st. nicholas never filled them,
he just watched, holding his
big wooden staff while mom stopped
on the way home from work
to buy candy at cvs;
pixie sticks & peanut butter cups.

she didn't need to do that;
i always wonder what moved her.

not many people in kutztown, pennsylvania
celebrate st. nicholas day but we did.

this year when i put my shoes out
on the porch, all ten pairs of them,
i feel greedy.

st. nicholas comes & fills them
with twigs
(what the bad children get).

magic tricks

st. simon the apostle was sawn in half longitudinally
or at least that's what some records indicate.
magicians perform the same trick, it's always simon in
the box. often, she takes the form of a woman. this is
how she wishes she would have lived; lovely & in a sparkly silver dress.
the magician cuts a different direction, though.
across the waist instead of
between the eyes. the way simon was martyred
broke her into two people both girls, beautiful &
with dirty blonde hair. simon was not much of a preacher or
really a good follower. magicians always remind her of
jesus. i ask her what I would become
if she sawed me in half. between the eyes.
she thinks I might divide,
hemorrhage into thousands break into thousands of boys.

swim lessons

I.

escape persecution by swimming.

II.

tie bricks to the crusades
& watch them sink deep into
the mediterranean.

>you will not need them.

III.

there are several ways to
learn how to swim,

one is to have
faith in god &
the another is to put your
trust in water

IV.

my swim instructor
was a pilot & his blue plane

made scar lines across the sky
in kutztown.

the backstroke made me feel like
a helicopter,

like the one that air-lifted
bodies away from
the town.

V.

& there was st. adjutor,
still escaping.

in every river & stream
& ocean & lake i pass
i see him swimming, farther
& farther away from god.

VI.

you can run from god,
fairly easily, but not from water.

the ceiling of my room collects clouds
when i'm not careful.

VII.

st. adjutor will one
day arrive at an abbey in france
where he will go to be alone forever.

i hope he likes it there,
wrapped in a towel
& smelling like chlorine.

VIII.

there's nowhere
to swim when it's december
& the pools are full of saints.

IX.

st. adjutor does the breast stroke
in my bathtub
& i get in with him.

i'm surprised that there's enough room
for the both of us.

between breaths he tells
me that i will never
know what it was
like to fight in the crusades.

i believe him & i tell
he will never know what it's
like to live in a time where

the existence of your skin
is political.

he says we should save
such serious discussions
for a time when we
both have clothes on.

X.

we stop swimming for a second
to observe each other's nakedness.

i put his hand to the scars
on my chest & say
they're cloud trails.

some stations of the cross

13.
down,
a motion better than falling.
take *down*
the scarecrows in december,
the sugar from the shelf
the box of photographs
the crosses from the walls.

jesus is dead & we made
him into a porcelain doll.

he breaks easily.
he's angry at his father.
he throws stones only
at open windows.

heaven's house is empty,
just god at a long kitchen
table, carving a turkey
for no one.

14.
lay
& laid. on a stone bed
where all sons go to sleep.

here we have moses & cain
& abel & elisha & jonah &
john & john & john.

i put jesus in a cardboard
box, the same one we used
to burry a dead chicken
when i was ten.

jesus looks a lot like
that chicken. stiff from
rigor mortis & the muscles
under his tan skin so defined.

i say, *i'm sorry jesus,*
i'm sorry.

15.
rise
good & hard & fast.

rise like cock if you must,
become a monument &
in the front lawn of your father's house.

beat the mail box with a baseball bat,
burn the junk mail out of spite.

in the yard i go looking for
the dead chicken, digging & digging,

i only find crosses. all sorts of crosses,
rosaries & little statues.

i do not find the chicken.
maybe there never was a chicken,
only jesus resting for a moment
in a cardboard box.

he plays in his father's yard,
a teenager now. he puts on
red heels to make god angry.

i watch him from
the sidewalk.

it's sunday.

i played elijah in my church's vacation bible school theater

i say / when all else fails / there will be caves

to return to. / great worlds of rock / to crawl inside

where god's voice / is eroded & soft. / where darkness

eats all colors, / pigment viscous / thick tongue.

elijah hid here / & i search / for his face.

stone / & stone / & stone.

gravel under nails. / in the nothing / i watch him.

he runs his / hands across the / walls,

cultivating callouses. / in here we will / cull our bodies

until they are part / of the cave & / call with our voices

until they are the same / quiet mouths / that god used once.

any day now / i will touch him / & not recognize

him as human. / i will speak to him / & he will think

i'm god. / we'll both be / beautiful stones.

acknowledgments

"vows of virginity" & "temples of venus"
    A Whore's Manifesto, Fall 2019
"sacrament I" & "sacrament III"
    POETRY, March 2020
"bride of Christ"
    Cobalt, Spring 2019
"magic tricks"
    Havik, Spring 2019

Robin Gow is the author of the chapbook *Honeysuckle*. Their poetry has been published in *POETRY*, *Thin Air*, and *45th Parallel* and has won prizes from Brooklyn Poets, Negative Capability Press, and *Fearsome Creatures Magazine*. They is the Editor-at-Large for *Village of Crickets*, Managing Editor at *The Nasiona* and Social Media Coordinator for *Oyster River Pages*. Their chapbook, *A Museum For That Which No Longer Exists* was runner up in *New Delta Review's* 2019 chapbook contest and their chapbook, *Some Metaphors Are Self-Inflicted* was a finalist for *Glass Poetry's* 2019 chapbook contest. They is an out-and-proud, genderqueer person passionate about LGBTQIA+ issues. They also runs a non-profit for transgender youth and does LGBTQIA+ inclusivity trainings at schools, colleges, and health care systems across the country. They is a graduate student and professor at Adelphi University. They is the founder of Gender Reveal Party, a trans and queer reading series in New York City.
.